Far Out, Brussel Sprout!

A first collection of
Australian children's
chants and rhymes

Compiled by June Factor

Illustrated by Peter Viska

BROLLY BOOKS

Published by Brolly Books
[an independent Australian publisher]
Suite 330, 45 Glenferrie Road
Malvern Victoria 3144 Australia
www.brollybooks.com

First published by Oxford University Press in 1983.
Reprinted 1984 (three times), 1985 (four times)
1986 (five times), 1987 (twice), 1988 (three times),
1989 (twice), 1990 (twice), 1992.
Second edition published by Hodder Children's books, 1995.
Reprinted 1996, 1997, 1998 (twice), 2000, 2001
This third edition first published 2004.
Reprinted 2005, 2007, 2008

Copyright this collection (c) June Factor, 1983
Copyright illustrations (c) Peter Viska, 1983

All rights reserved. No part of this book may be stored
or reproduced by any process whatsoever except as permitted
under the Copyright Act of Australia without the prior
written permission of the Publishers.
Printed in China.

ISBN 1877035 27 0 ·

Cataloguing-in-Publication data is available
through the National Library of Australia.

For Children

This books belongs to you in a very special way: it's yours because you — together with many other children — have written it. Well, not exactly written it, but made it up. Everything in this book comes from the games, rhymes, riddles and jokes that Australian children make up and teach each other when they play together. All I've done is to write down what you say.

This means that you will know a lot of what is in this book already. But sometimes the words of a rhyme *you* say will not be quite the same as the rhyme in this book. That's because every group of children play and chant and joke in their own way. The rhymes used in one school are not always the same as those found in another. That's one good thing about this book — it can introduce you to rhymes you've never heard before.

Of course, I couldn't fit every rhyme that Australian children say into this book, but I would like to hear about the way *you* play in your school and street, and about the rhymes, riddles, jokes and games you know. You can write to me at the address at the bottom of this page and tell me what you do when you and your friends get together. Perhaps we'll get so many letters that we'll have to publish another book!

June Factor
PO Box 1063
Ivanhoe Victoria 3079

Acknowledgements

The material in this book is drawn largely from the archives of the Australian Children's Folklore Collection, now housed at Museum Victoria. I am grateful to the Institute of Early Childhood Development (now subsumed into the University of Melbourne) for its support, and to the many students from the Institute who collected games, rhymes and other playground lore from children. My special thanks to Gwenda Davey and Heather Russell for their encouragement and practical assistance.

This book is dedicated to all the
- Ch'ings
- Harrys
- Irinas
- Leons
- Deirdres
- Robertos
- Eleanors and
- Nicks

of Australia.

Man fat
Top hat
Fell flat
Squashed hat.

Quickly, quickly, I feel sickly.
Hasten, hasten, get the basin.
Ker plop!
Get the mop!

Man in car
Went to bar
Feeling nifty
Doing fifty
Hit a pole
Poor old soul
Doctor's fee
Cemetery.

Mummy, mummy, what's that stuff?
It looks like strawberry jam.
Tut, tut, my child,
It's just papa
Run over by a tram.

Nobody loves me, everybody hates me,
I'm going out to eat some worms.
Big fat juicy ones, long slim slimy ones,
Itsy, bitsy, fuzzy wuzzy worms.
First you eat their heads off,
Then you suck their gizzards out,
See how they squiggle and squirm!
Big fat juicy ones, long slim slimy ones,
Itsy, bitsy, fuzzy wuzzy worms.

Over my teeth
Over my tongue
Look out stomach here it comes!

Ooey gooey custard,
Green maggot pie.
Four dogs' gizzards
And one cat's eye.
Four blood sandwiches
Coated on thick,
All washed down
With a cup of cold sick.

Polly on the railway road,
Picking up stones,
Along came an engine
And broke poor Polly's bones.
'Oh!' said Polly, 'that's not fair.'
'Poof!' said the engine,
'I don't care!'

Ooey Gooey was a worm,
A big fat worm was he.
He sat upon a railway track,
A train he did not see.
The train came roaring round the bend
The driver gave a squeal,
The guard got out his pocket knife
And scraped him off the wheel.
Ooey Gooey!

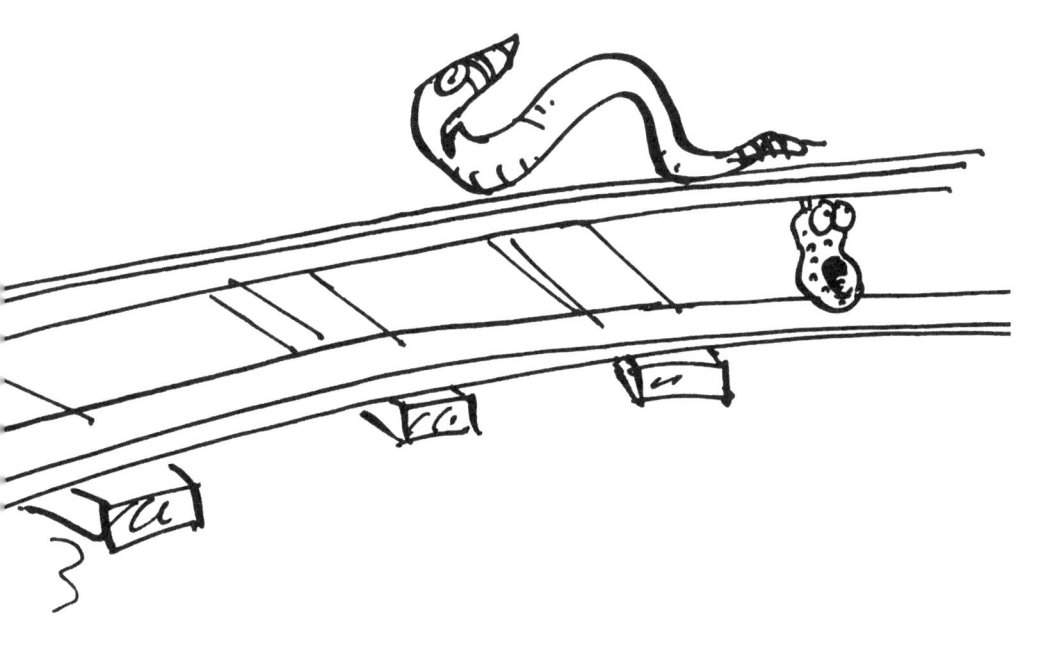

A peanut sat on a railway track,
Its heart was all a-flutter.
Around the corner came the 4.15 —
Bang! Crash! Peanut butter!

Sausage dog
Busy street
Motor car
Mince meat.

Nellie Bly caught a fly,
Tied it to a string.
String broke, cut its throat,
Poor little thing.

One, two, three,
Mother caught a flea.
Put it in a teapot
And had a cup of tea.

The flea jumped out,
Mother gave a shout,
In came daddy with his shirt hanging out.

Tit for tat
Butter for fat
If you kick my dog
I'll kick your cat.

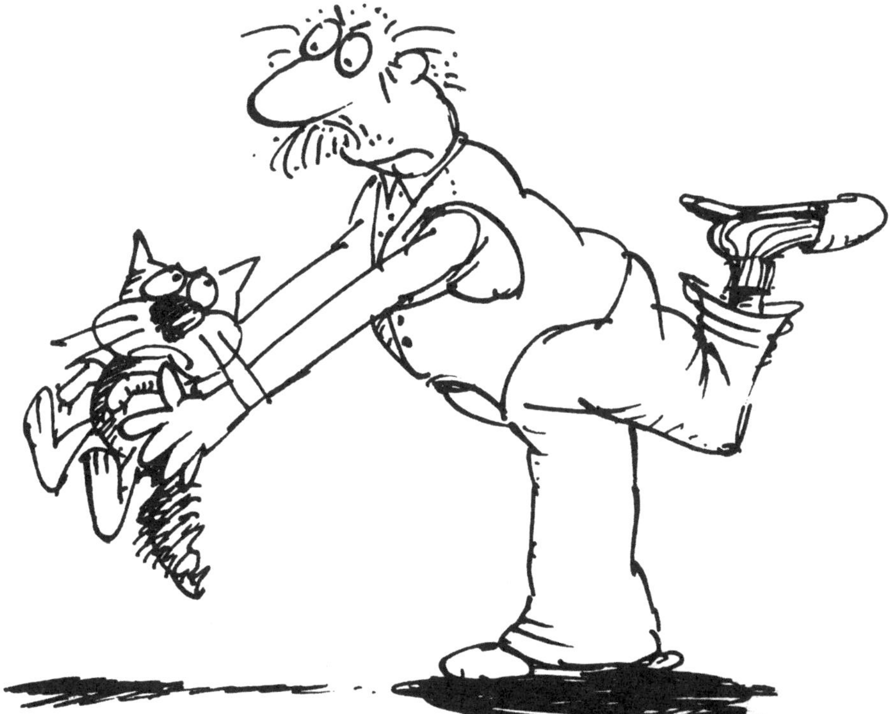

There was an old man from Wonthaggi
Who climbed up a tree for a maggie;
The maggie let fly
And whitewashed his eye
That poor old man from Wonthaggi.

Of all the birds I'd like to be
I'd like to be a sparra,
So I could sit on Princes Bridge
And help to fill the Yarra.

There was a little boy scout
Of one good deed could boast:
He saved a little sardine
From falling off his toast.

A rabbit has a shiny nose,
I'll tell you why, my friend:
Because his little powder puff
Is on the other end.

The night was dark and stormy,
The dunny light was dim,
I heard a crash and then a splash —
By gosh! He's fallen in.

The night was dark and stormy,
The billy-goat was blind,
He ran into a barbed wire fence
And tore his bare behind.

The lightning crashed,
The thunder roared
Around the homestead station.
The little pig curled up his tail
And ran to save his bacon.

She danced across the ballroom floor,
Her dress it was fantastic.
All of a sudden she rushed for the door —
You can't trust Coles' elastic.

'You're a nut.'

'Thank you. Nuts grow on trees,
trees are nature,
and nature is beautiful.'

You are so low that, if there was a car on a bridge
and under the bridge there was a rock
and under the rock there was a stone
and under the stone there was a snail
and under the snail there was a bull ant
and under the bull ant there was a flea,
you could walk under the flea!

Hope your chooks turn to emus
and kick your dunny doors down.

If your brain was made of water you'd be a walking drought.
Take a long walk off a short pier.

Colin and a monkey
Were sitting on a rail.
The only difference I could see —
The monkey had a tail.

Susan and her donkey
Were sitting on a fence.
The only difference I could see —
The donkey had more sense.

Giddy giddy gout,
Your shirt's hanging out.
Ten miles in,
Ten miles out.

Sticky beak, treacle nose,
Lolly legs and ice-cream toes.

If you think you're sweet,
Take off your shoes
And smell your feet.

I'm an Australian born and bred,
Long in the leg
And thick in the head.

Little Miss Muffet
Sat on her tuffet,
Eating her curds and whey.
Along came a spider
Who sat down beside her
And little Miss Muffet said:
'Buzz off, hairy legs!'

Hickory, dickory, dock,
Two mice ran up the clock.
The clock struck one,
And the other one got away.

Mary, Mary, quite contrary,
How does your garden grow?
Up, stupid!

Mary, Mary, quite contrary,
How does your garden grow?
With silver bells and cockle shells
And one lousy little petunia.

Sweet tooth Jenny
Now hasn't any.

Far out, brussel sprout!

Jingle bells
Batman smells
Robin ran away,
The batmobile lost its wheel
And landed in the bay.

Jingle bells
Robin smells
Batman flew away,
Lost his pants while over France
And found them in Bombay.

Twinkle, twinkle little star,
Daddy drives a rotten car.
Press the button, pull the choke,
Off we go in a cloud of smoke.
Twinkle, twinkle little star,
Daddy drives a rotten car.

Simple Simon met a pieman
Going to a fair.
Said Simple Simon to the pieman,
'What have you got there?'
'Pies, stupid!'

Baa, baa black sheep,
Have you any wool?
Yes sir, yes sir,
Three bags full.
One for the jumpers,
And one for the smocks,
And one for the little boy
With holes in his socks.

Little Jack Horner sat in a corner,
Eating his Christmas Pie.
He put in his thumb
And pulled out a plum
And squirted the juice in his eye.

Ding, dong, dell,
Pussy's in the well.
If you don't believe it,
Go and have a smell.

Happy birthday to you,
You live in the zoo,
You look like a monkey
And you smell like one too.

Mary had a little lamb,
Her father shot it dead
And now it goes to school with her
Between two chunks of bread.

Mary had a little lamb.
The doctor fainted.

42

Mary had a little lamb,
She also had a bear.
I often saw her little lamb
But I never saw her bare.

Mary had a little lamb,
Ronny had a pup.
Fred had an alligator
That ate the others up.

Mary had a little lamb,
She kept it in the closet
And every time she let it out
It left a small deposit.

Mary had a little chook,
She kept it in a bucket
'Cause every time she let it out
The rooster used to pluck it.

Humpty Dumpty sat on a chair,
Eating ripe bananas.
Where do you think he put the skins?
Down his new pyjamas!

Humpty Dumpty sat on the wall,
Humpty Dumpty had a great fall,
All the King's horses and all the King's men,
Had omelets for breakfast.

Roses are red,
Violets are blue,
Cashews are nuts
And so are you.

Roses are red,
Spiders are black,
Don't look now
But there's one on your back.

Roses are red,
Emeralds are green,
My face is funny
But yours is a scream.

Roses are red,
Violets are blue,
You look like a cow,
Moo, moo, moooo.

Roses are red,
Violets are blue,
I have a boyfriend,
And so do you.
Tell your mum to hold her tongue
'Cause she had one when she was young.
Tell your dad to do the same
'Cause he was the one
Who changed your mum's name.

Roses are red,
Violets are blue,
The sound of raindrops
Reminds me of you:
Drip, drip, drip.

Roses are red,
Violets are blue,
The sound of bells
Reminds me of you:
NING NONG *NING* NONG *NING* NONG.

Roses are red,
Violets are blue,
Onions stink,
And aren't geraniums a funny colour?

[*To the tune of* John Brown's Body . . .]

He joined the parachuters for the fancy uniform,
He joined the parachuters for the fancy uniform,
He joined the parachuters for the fancy uniform,
And he ain't going to jump no more!

Chorus
Glory, glory hallelujah,
Glory, glory hallelujah,
Glory, glory hallelujah,
And he ain't going to jump no more!

They took him in a plane for more than 40,000 feet . . .
He jumped from 40,000 feet without a parachute . . .
He landed on the target like a lump of strawberry jam . . .
They scraped him off the target with a rusty razorblade . . .
They put him in an envelope and sent him home to mum
His mum wasn't home so they fed him to the dog .
The dog didn't like him so they threw him in the bin . . .

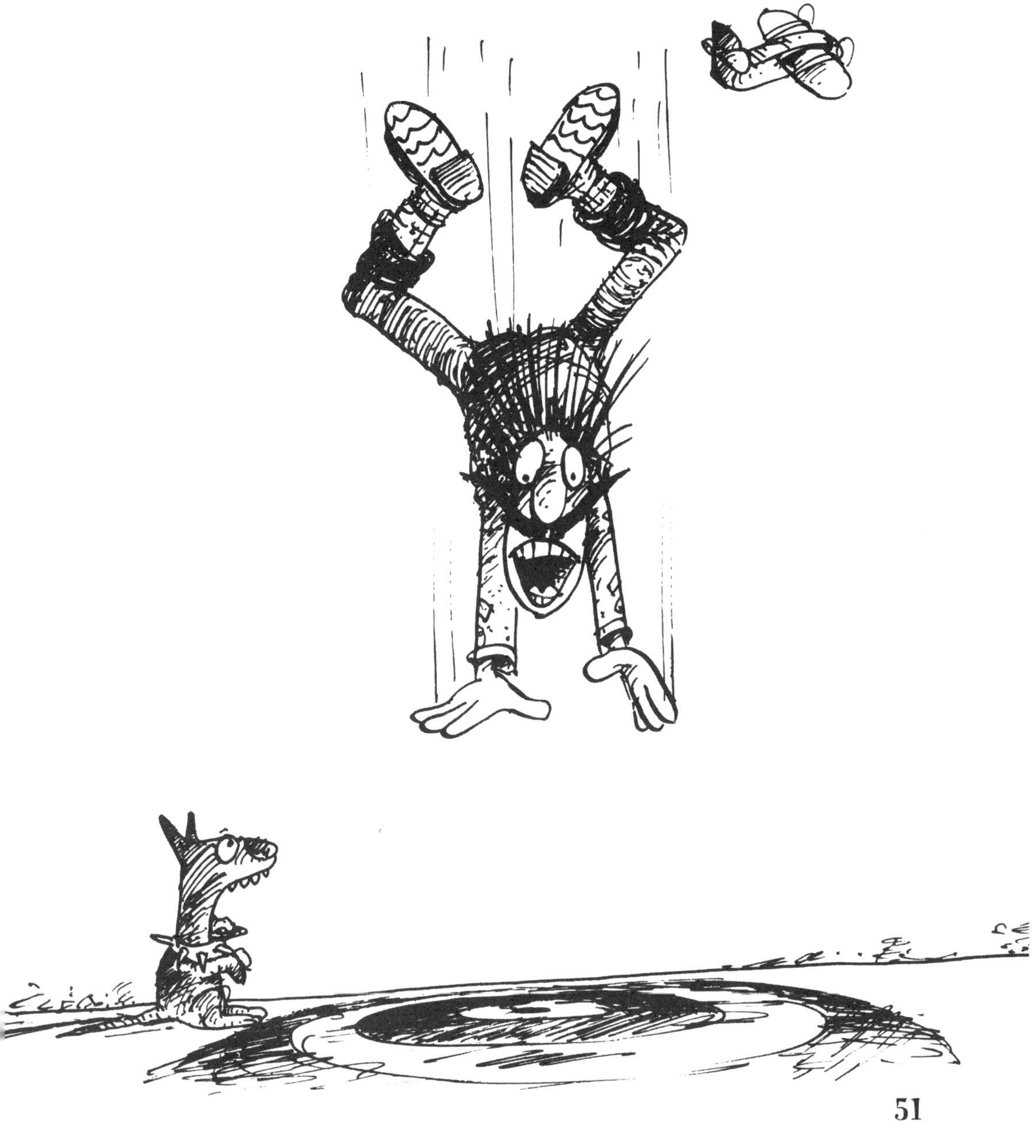

Daisy, Daisy, where's Uncle Jim?
He's in the bathtub learning how to swim.
First he does the breaststroke
Then he does the dive,
Over goes the bathtub
With Uncle Jim inside.

Daisy, Daisy, how is Uncle Tim?
He's in the bathtub learning how to swim.
First he does the backstroke
Then he does the side,
Now he's down the plughole
Swimming against the tide.

Glory, glory hallelujah!
Teacher hit me with the ruler.
I hit her on the chin
With a rotten mandarin
And her teeth came marching out.

Po Karie Karie Arn-na
I found a rotten ban-ana
I threw it at the teacher
And it made her cry.
Now the teacher said, 'Come he-re,'
But I said, 'No fe-ar,'
So she took me by the e-ar,
And made me cry.

God save our biscuit tin,
Don't let the rats get in,
God save our tin.
If they do get in,
Throw the Ratsac in,
Just to save our biscuit tin,
God save our tin.

Good King Wenceslas
Went to town
In a Mini Minor,
Crashed into an atom bomb
And ended up in China.

We three kings of Orient are,
Sitting on a rubber cigar.
It was loaded and exploded —
Silent night!

Row, row, row your boat
Gently down the stream,
If you see a crocodile,
Don't forget to scream.

Oh, dear! What can the matter be?
Three old ladies got locked in the lavatory.
They stayed there from Monday to Saturday,
Nobody knew they were there.

'Doctor, doctor, I feel like a curtain.'
'For heaven's sake, man,
Pull yourself together!'

'Doctor, doctor, I feel like a dog.'
'How long has this been going on?'
'Since I was a pup.'

You remind me of a man.	What man?
A hoodoo.	Who do?
You do. / What?	Remind me of a man.

How many cans can a cannibal nibble,
If a cannibal can nibble cans?
As many cans as a cannibal can,
If a cannibal can nibble cans.

A wonderful bird is the pelican,
His beak can hold more than his belly can.

Spring is sprung,
The grass is riz,
I wonder where the birdie is?
They say the bird is on the wing,
But I say the wing is on the bird.

I've never seen a purple cow
I hope I never see one,
But I can tell you even now,
I'd rather see than be one.

They speak of the state of the weather,
They talk of the birds that sing,
But to sit down quick on a red hot brick
Is the sign of an early spring.

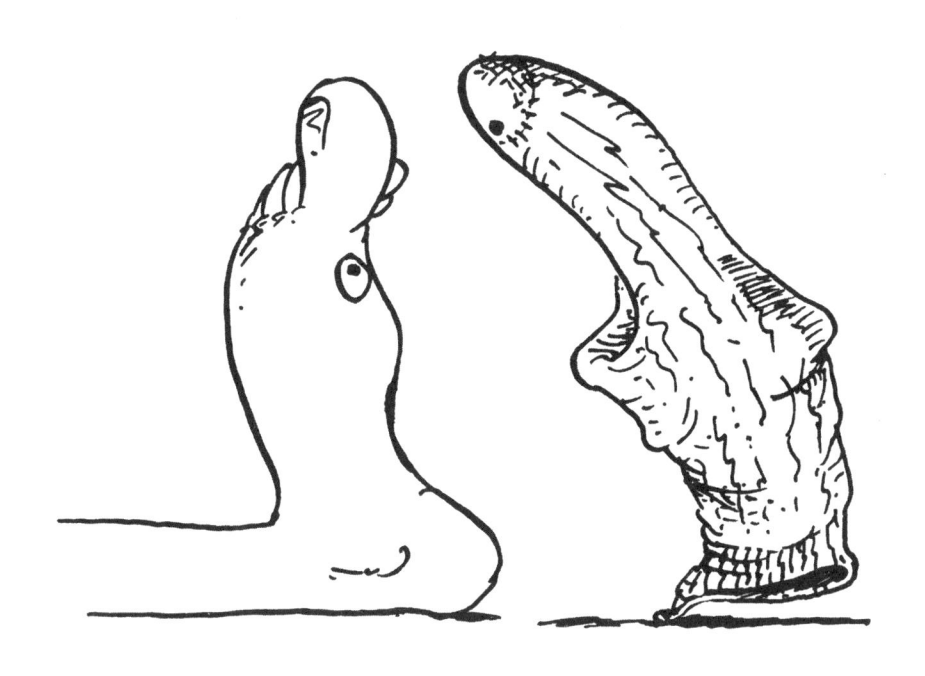

Said one toe to the sock,
'Let me through, let me through!'
Said the sock to the toe,
'I'll be darned if I do!'

Way down south where bananas grow,
A grasshopper stepped on an elephant's toe.
Elephant said with tears in his eyes:
'Pick on someone your own size!'

The Lord said unto Moses:
'Come forth.'
But he slipped on a banana skin
And came fifth.

One dark day in the middle of the night,
Two dead men got up to fight.
The blind man went to see fair play,
The dumb man went to shout 'hooray'.
Back to back they faced each other,
Drew their swords and shot each other!

I went to the pictures tomorrow,
And took a front seat at the back.
I fell from the floor to the ceiling,
And hurt the front part of my back.

Ladies and gentlemen,
I come before you to stand behind you,
To tell you something I know nothing about.
On Monday, which is Good Friday,
There will be a mothers' meeting for fathers only.
Admission is free,
You pay at the door.
Bring your own seats,
We'll sit on the floor.

I dreamt that I died
And to heaven did go.
'Where do you come from?'
They all wanted to know.
When I said 'Melbourne'
Didn't they stare!
'Come in,' they all cried,
'You're the first one from there.'

Inky, pinky, alligator winky,
Oxtail, out!
I saw a butcher boy
Riding on a saveloy.

Inky pinky ponky
Daddy bought a donkey,
Donkey died
Daddy cried
Inky pinky ponky.

Inky pinky ponky
Donkey bought a daddy,
Daddy died
Donkey cried
Inky pinky ponky.

Inky pinky panky
Daddy bought a hanky,
Hanky tore
Daddy swore
Inky pinky panky.

A man walked into a beer bottle shop
And asked for a bottle of beer.
Where's your money?
In my pocket.
Where's your pocket?
I forgot it.
Please step out.

Eenie meenie macka racka,
Rare rye dominacka,
Chickapop, alollipop,
Rang pang puss.
Penny on the water,
Tuppence on the sea,
Threepence on the whirly whirly,
You're not he.

Eenie meenie
makka rakka
rear rie
damma nakka
chiko poppo
rang pang push.

Onery overy ickery am,
Fillisy follisy nickols ham,
Queeby qwawby Irish mawby,
Ticklum tacklum buck,
For a rotten dotten dirty dish clout,
Out, boys, *out!*

My mother said,
I never should
Play with the gypsies
In the wood.
If I did, she would say:
'Naughty girl to disobey.'
Disobey one, disobey two,
Disobey cock-a-doodle-do.
The grass was green, the sky was blue,
The cow in the meadow said *moo, moo, moo.*

Ooza Tooza,
Vocka Tooza,
Vee Vi Vo
Vanish!

I had a little brother
His name was Tiny Tim,
I put him in the bathtub
To teach him how to swim.

He drank up all the water,
He ate up all the soap,
He died last night
With a bubble in his throat.

In came the doctor,
In came the nurse,
In came the lady
With the alligator purse.

'Dead,' said the doctor,
'Dead,' said the nurse,
'Dead,' said the lady
With the alligator purse.

Out went the doctor,
Out went the nurse,
Out went the lady
With the alligator purse.

Mother, mother, I feel sick,
Send for the doctor,
Quick, quick, quick.
In comes the doctor,
In comes the nurse,
In comes the lady
With the alligator purse.
'It's the end,' says the doctor,
'It's the end,' says the nurse,
'It's the end,' says the lady
With the alligator purse.

Oliver Crumble lost his shoe
In the battle of Waterloo.
He went, I went all the way,
Singing tra, la, la,
Bim, bom, bay.

Sally over the water
Sally over the sea,
Sally broke the milk bottle
And blamed it on to me.
Sally told ma,
Ma told pa,
Sally got a scolding —
Ha, ha, ha!

Inch, pinch, pear, plum,
I smell Tom Thumb.
Tom Thumb in the woods,
Making friends
   with Robin Hood.
Robin Hood in the cellar,
Making love to Rockefeller,
Rockefeller dressed in yeller
Turns around like this.

Ice-cream, jelly, apple tart,
Tell me the name of your sweetheart.
A, B, C, D, E . . . Eric
Eric, Eric come to tea,
Eric, Eric marry me,
Yes, no, yes, no, yes, no.

82

Jelly on the plate, jelly on the plate,
Wiggle, woggle, wiggle, woggle,
Jelly on the plate.
Sausages in the pan, sausages in the pan,
Turn them over, turn them over,
Sausages in the pan.
Jam on the shelf, jam on the shelf,
Pull it down, pull it down, jam on the shelf.
Pennies on the floor, pennies on the floor,
Pick them up, pick them up, pennies on the floor.
Dirt in the room, dirt in the room,
Sweep it out, sweep it out, dirt in the room.
Robbers in the house, robbers in the house,
Kick them out, kick them out, robbers in the house.
Apples on the tree, apples on the tree,
Pick them off, pick them off, apples on the tree.
Ants in your pants, ants in your pants,
Scratch them out, scratch them out,
Ants in your pants.

I was going to the country,
I was going to the fair,
I met a señorita
With the curls in her hair.
Shake señorita, shake it all you can,
Shake señorita, till you find a handsome man.
Rumble to the bottom,
Rumble to the top,
Turn around, turn around,
Turn around, *stop*.

Not last night but the night before
Twenty-four robbers came knocking at my door.
As I came out to let them in
They stole some money from the biscuit tin,
And this is what they said:
Spanish lady turn around,
Spanish lady touch the ground,
Spanish lady do the kicks,
Spanish lady do the splits.

I'm a cup and saucer, floating on the water,
Along came a big wave and pushed me over.
I'm a little Dutch girl, dressed in blue,
These are the things that I must do:
Salute to the captain,
Curtsy to the queen,
And show my knickers to the football team.

I saw my cup and saucer
Floating in the water,
In came a whale
And turned it over.
When I say two
Touch your shoe.
When I say four
Touch the floor.
When I say six
Do the splits.
When I say eight
Stand up straight.
When I say ten
Do it again.
Two, four, six, eight, ten!

Granny in the kitchen
Doing a bit of stitchin',
Along comes a bogey man
And kicks her out.
Bogey man in the kitchen
Doing a bit of stitchin',
Along comes granny
And kicks him out.

Elvis Presley is a star,
S–T–A–R.
He can do the go-go,
He can do the twist,
He can do the twirly whirl
And he can do the splits.

Firecracker, firecracker,
Boom, boom, boom.
Firecracker, firecracker,
Boom, boom, boom.
The boys have got the muscles
The teacher's got the brains,
But the girls have got the sexy legs
So they win the game.

All in together girls,
This fine weather.
I see a nanny-goat
Peeping up my petticoat,
Swish, swash, fire!

Koala bear, koala bear, touch the ground
Koala bear, koala bear, turn around
Koala bear, koala bear, climb up the stairs
Koala bear, koala bear, say your prayers
Koala bear, koala bear, switch off the light
Koala bear, koala bear, say good night.

Salami, salami,
Hickory salami.
Hands up,
Stick 'em up,
Don't forget to pick 'em up,
And out you go.

Two little sausages frying in a pan,
One went sizzle
And the other went *bang!*

Andy Pandy, sugar and candy,
French, almond, raisin, rock.
Bread and butter for your supper,
All your mother's got.

Turn the rope
Turn the rope
Turn the rope over.
Marigolds and hollyhocks,
Buttercups and clover.

All in
　with a bottle of gin,
All out
　with a bottle of stout,
All under
　with a bottle of thunder,
All over
　with a bottle of clover.
In, out, over, under.

Johnny and Jane and Jack and Lou,
Butler's Stairs through Woolloomooloo,
Woolloomooloo, and 'cross the Domain,
Round the Block, and home again!
Heigh, ho! Tipsy toe,
Give us a kiss and away we go.

Don't leave this rope empty
Don't kiss a boy until you're twenty.

A sailor went to sea, sea, sea,
To see what he could see, see, see,
But all that he could see, see, see,
Was miles of deep blue sea, sea, sea.

My name is . . .
Anti, Anti,
Chickidee, Chickidee,
Oony, Oony,
Oompapa.
Walla, Walla,
Whisky,
Chinese sauce.

Mary Mack, dressed in black,
Silver buttons down her back.
She likes coffee
She likes tea
She likes sitting on her daddy's knee.

One morning I awoke
And I saw upon my wall
The beetles and the bedrocks
Were having a game of ball.
The score was six to nothing
The beetles were ahead,
The bedrocks scored a homing run
Which knocked me out of bed, bed, bed,
Which knocked me out of BED!

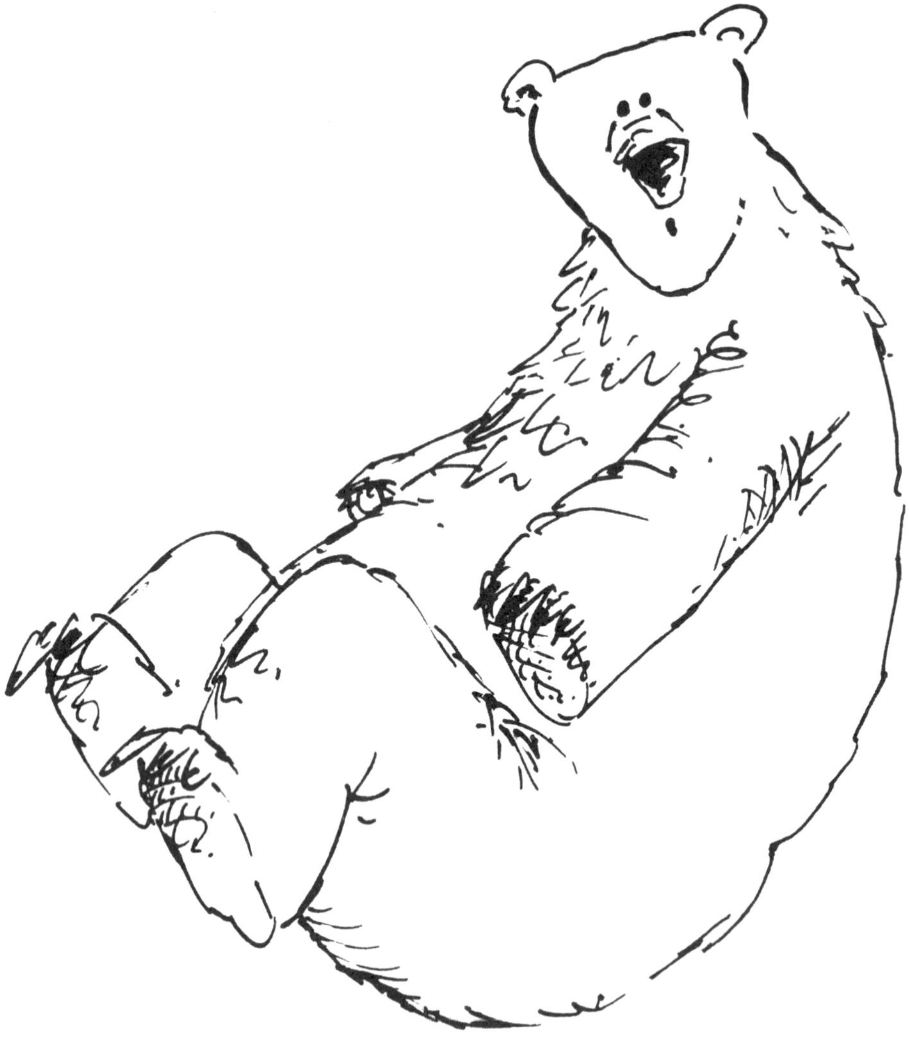

Hello sir, hello, sir,
Meet you at the show, sir.
No, sir. Why, sir?
Because I've got a cold, sir.

Where'd you get the cold, sir?
At the north pole, sir.
What were you doing there, sir?
Catching polar bears, sir.

How many did you catch, sir?
One sir, two sir, three sir, four sir, five sir,
Six sir, seven sir, eight sir, nine sir, ten sir.
All the rest were dead sir.

How did they die, sir?
Eating apple pie, sir.
What was in the pie, sir?
A big fat fly, sir.

What was in the fly, sir?
A big fat germ, sir.
What was in the germ, sir?
A big fat you, sir!

Two in a hammock ready to kiss,
Then all of a sudden they landed like this.

They stood on the porch at midnight,
Their lips were tightly pressed,
The old man gave the signal
And the bulldog did the rest.

When you get married
Happy may you be
Blessed with little ones
One, two and three.
One to wash the dishes
One to scrub the floor
One to rock the cradle
In case there's any more.

Mr   Miss
Meet   Kiss
More   Kisses
Mr   Mrs

Two in a car
Two little kisses,
Two weeks later
Mr and Mrs.

Some kiss beneath the apple tree
Some kiss beneath the rose,
But we all know that the right place to kiss
Is an inch below the nose.

They walked the lane together,
The sky was dotted with stars.
They reached the rails together,
He lifted up the bars.
She neither smiled nor thanked him
Because she knew not how,
For he was only the farmer's boy
And she was the jersey cow!

Beware of boys with eyes of brown,
They kiss you once and turn you down.
Beware of boys with eyes of green,
They kiss you once and then you scream.
Beware of boys with eyes of grey,
They kiss you once and turn away.
Beware of boys with eyes of blue,
They kiss you once and ask for two.

Never kiss at the garden gate,
Love is blind but the neighbours ain't.

Two lovers stood on Sydney bridge,
Her lips were all a-quiver.
He kissed her
And her leg fell off
And floated down the river.

1 1 was a racehorse.
2 2 was 1 2.
1 1 1 1 race and
2 2 1 1 2.

2 Ys U R
2 Ys U B
I C U R
2 Ys 4 Me.

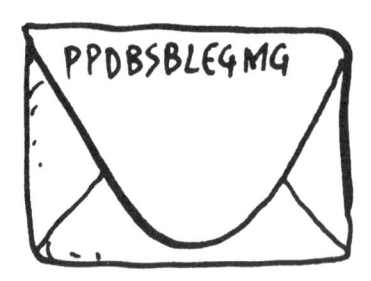

PPDBSBLE4MG

Postman, postman,
Don't be slow.
Be like Elvis,
Go, man, go!

N E 1 4 10 S?

[*Read in the direction of the arrows*]

↑ down ↓ and   ↑ you   ↓ if   ↑ find ↓ you   ↑ you   ↓ will
  and   you   love   you   I   love   for   be
  up   will   I   love   if   me   love   forgot.
  Read   see   that   me.   And   not   my

Washing day at the nudist camp.

103

War must cease
Or all life ceases.
Live in peace
Or die in pieces.

My ♥ 4 u.

There are gold ships
There are silver ships
But the best ship
Is friendship.

Make new friends
But keep the old,
New friends are silver,
Old friends are gold.

See you later alligator
In a while crocodile.
Not tonight vegemite,
Oo roo, kangaroo.

Ashes to ashes,
Dust to dust,
If Lillee don't get you
Thommo must.

A little mouse crawled up the wall,
Ladies and gentlemen, that is all.

By hook or by crook
I'll be last in this book!

For Adults

This book contains a small selection from the vast number of Australian children's rhymes. Like children everywhere, youngsters in this country — whatever their skin colour, language, religion or class — spend time playing together. Often this play is spontaneous, 'made up on the spot', but a great deal is traditional, passed from child to child in a long chain that stretches back hundreds of years and across continents and cultures.

Children play for fun. In the process of play, particularly rule-governed play, children learn and practise skills, and test themselves physically, socially and intellectually. The traditional games of the schoolground are as important to children's development as formal lessons in the classroom.

Many adults, especially teachers, are interested in this play and in the accompanying verbal lore. They would like to be able to draw upon such a prolific and inventive repertoire to enrich their work with children. However, thoughtful observers have hesitated to intrude on an area so clearly of, by, and for, children.

We do not know what long-term effects the intrusion of adults into children's traditional play may have. I believe we are wise to be cautious. The suggestions for adult involvement which follow are based on a careful assessment of the risks, and are prefaced by the warning that neither compulsion nor authoritarianism has any place in the traditional play of children. Moreover, facets of children's lore may be quite inappropriate for classroom use. Nonetheless there is much that can be accommodated comfortably within a flexible school programme — one taught by teachers who acknowledge children as the authority in this field.

The rhymes in this book are often witty, full of puns, parody, alliteration and other poetic devices. They are richly rhythmic and cleverly rhymed. After nursery rhymes, they are the major source of poetry for many children. Adults who wish to avoid the cry of 'Oh, not poetry!' common in Australian schools might find these rhymes helpful — for chanting, singing, adapting, futher parodying — but not for solemn dissection!

'Learning by heart' comes easily with these rhymes, and children will happily invent and play with linguistic forms, as they do already in the playground. To encourage such activity is to enhance children's verbal dexterity and their overall grasp of their mother tongue (or of their second tongue, as in the case of many children of immigrants). What is more, the children become the teachers — which is good for confidence and encouraging for everyone.

Such a collection should also prove of value to the so-called reluctant reader, not only because of its liveliness and humour, but also because it contains largely 'known' material. It is almost impossible for a child *not* to be able to read this book!

A number of these rhymes are used to accompany a movement game: counting out, skipping, hand-clapping and ball-bouncing. The physical co-ordination, flexibility, patience and endurance required for many of these games suggest how strenuously, seriously — and co-operatively — children play. It is likely that children who play such games regularly are exercising more thoroughly than is possible in the usual physical education programme. Perhaps if adults deliberately encourage the playing of such games (tactfully — they are, after all, the collective 'property' of children) the physical well-being of primary school children could be improved. The games could also act as a healthy antidote to the highly competitive and sometimes aggressive adult sports that are often introduced to children at a very early age.

These rhymes are evidence of children's interest in the world around them, of their curiosity about love and sex, politics, television and sport, schools and teachers, religion and nationality. This curiosity, this fundamental need to know and understand, forms the basis for all learning, and offers the perceptive teacher a guide to children's preoccupations and points of view.

The rhymes have been carefully selected to include material originating from all over Australia, and collected from children of various ethnic groups. It is hoped that such diversity will encourage recognition of the commonality of childhood, and help to break down old prejudices and antagonisms. The collection is far from comprehensive, as many forthright expressions of sexual interest and racial and religious prejudice have been omitted, but it can be seen as a limited but authentic guide to the thinking of pre-pubescent children.

Many children would gain much pleasure and benefit from making their own collections of rhymes — and games, jokes, riddles, tall stories, and autograph album entries. The folklore of childhood is a magnificently rich resource, and adults who are careful not to 'take over' can share in its delights.

June Factor
1983

Far out, brussel sprout!